Why the Sea Is Salty

A Philippine Legend

Retold by Dot Meharry

Illustrated by Paolo Lim

Text and illustrations © Pearson Australia, 2012.
(a division of Pearson Australia Group Pty Ltd)

Text by Dot Meharry.
Illustrated by Paolo Lim.

First published in 2012 by Pearson Australia.
This edition of *Why the Sea Is Salty* is published by Pearson
Education Inc. by arrangement with Pearson Australia. All rights
reserved. Printed in Mexico.

ISBN-13: 978-0-328-83293-4
ISBN-10:   0-328-83293-6

6   17

Contents

Chapter 1

Salt

Long ago, the water in the sea was just like the rain that falls from the clouds and waters the earth. It was just like the underground water that flows into wells. It was just like the water in streams and rivers and lakes. It did not have any salt in it. It was clean and fresh, and there was plenty of it.

The people living on the islands in the Philippines would fill big pots with water from the sea and carry them back to their villages. They used the water for many things.

When they were thirsty, the villagers drank the water. They boiled their rice in it.

They gave the water to their pigs and chickens to drink. During the dry season, they watered their vegetable gardens with it. Their vegetables grew plump and sweet. The people on the islands were happy, and it seemed they had everything they needed.

But they did not have enough salt. Salt was important to the people and their way of life. They needed salt to keep healthy. They would mix salt and water together and bathe their wounds with it. They used salty water to wash their mouths and clean their teeth. The salt killed germs.

Sometimes, the people mixed salt with boiled rice and prawns to make a sauce. They let it bubble and stew until the shells of the prawns became red and soft in the salty mixture. The people liked salt in their food. It made their food tastier.

The people also needed salt to preserve food. They used salt to dry fish they caught, to stop them from going bad. They would cut the fish down the middle and open them up. Then they would rub salt into the raw flesh and hang them up in the sun to dry. The dried fish were good to eat.

All year round, the people needed salt. They took the fish they had salted and the different foods they had mixed with salt to the local markets. They sold them or swapped them for rice and other things they didn't have.

But what they needed the most was salt, and this could not be found at the markets. There was only one place they could get the salt they needed.

Chapter 2

The Giant

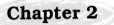

In those days, there was a giant who lived on one of the many islands in the Philippines. Deep under the ground on his island were large beds of salt.

The giant liked salt. He mined the salt and stored it inside a huge cave in the hills. Great piles of salt rose up to the roof like mountain peaks and filled the cave.

Luckily for the people, the giant was kind and generous. He happily shared his salt.

"Help yourself to as much as you need," he would say when they asked for salt.

The people were thankful that the giant let them get salt from his cave. To show they were grateful for his kindness, they always brought him gifts of food.

The giant looked forward to the people coming with food. He ate a lot and got tired of cooking his own meals.

He enjoyed the different foods they prepared for him, especially the sauce made with boiled rice and prawns. His favorites, though, were the many kinds of fish the people salted and dried in the sun.

The people were good at salting fish.
They used just the right amount of salt.

But it was not easy to get the
salt from the giant's cave. First,
the people traveled by boat to
his island. Then they walked
along a very steep path
through the jungle to get
to the cave. Vines and
twisted tree roots
grew across the path
and were like cleverly
set traps. If the people
were not careful, they
tripped and fell.

When they got to the
giant's cave and stepped inside,
there was just enough light for them to see
the great piles of salt. They would crouch
down and use their bare hands to scoop
salt into the bamboo baskets they brought
with them.

The smell of salt was so strong that it was hard to breathe in the cave. The villagers would try to fill the baskets as quickly as they could so they could get back into the fresh air.

The giant always waited outside the cave when people were getting salt. He knew how dangerous it was. If the people took too much salt from the bottom of the piles, they could cause a salt slide. They would be buried alive. He did not want anyone to get hurt while on his island.

With their baskets filled with salt, the people would lift the heavy loads onto their heads and carry them back down the steep path to their small boats on the shore. It was hard work, and usually only the strongest and fittest of the people were able to get the salt.

The giant worried as he watched the people sail back to their island. The heavy loads of salt made their small boats sit so low in the water that they were in danger of sinking.

Chapter 3

The Storm

One day, the villagers who lived on an island close to the giant's ran out of salt. Before the villagers could sail across the sea and get more, a storm blew in.

The wild wind raced across the sea, and white foam caps danced on the tops of big waves. The houses on their bamboo poles shook as the wind roared through the village. There was nothing the villagers could do but wait for the storm to pass.

Day after day, they waited. The villagers did not like being without salt. They had no salt to put in their food to make it tastier.

They had no salt to mix with water to bathe their wounds and kill germs.

"Who is brave enough to go and get some salt for us?" the villagers asked.

They listened to the roar of the wind. They looked at the big waves and were afraid.

"I know we need salt, but it's too dangerous to take the boats out yet," said a man, shaking his head. "Wait until the storm passes. Then we can sail to the giant's island to get more salt."

"Please, take me with you when you go," begged the man's young son. For years, the boy had wanted to go with his father to the giant's island and collect salt.

The man looked down at his son. "One day, I'll be an old man," he thought. "Then it will be my son's turn to get the salt for our family." He smiled at the boy.

"Yes, you can come," he said. "It's time you learned how to get the salt."

Chapter 4

The Boy

At last, the worst of the storm passed. Just as promised, the boy was allowed to sail to the giant's island with his father and some other villagers.

The boy was excited. He'd heard many stories about the giant and his cave. He wondered how many of these stories were really true.

The sea was still rough, and the small boat rocked and rolled in the waves. It wasn't long before the boy was seasick.

"There must be an easier way to get salt than this," he groaned.

"If there were, we would have thought of it long ago," his father answered.

The giant was waiting for them when they got to his island. He noticed the boy with his father. It had been a long time since he'd seen a child. Only adults ever came to get salt. The giant smiled at the boy staring up at him with wide eyes.

"We've got no dried squid for you today," called one villager. "We couldn't go fishing because of the storm."

"We don't have boiled rice mixed with prawns, either," said another.

The giant was disappointed. He'd been looking forward to the tasty food they usually brought him. He watched the villagers get their bamboo baskets out of their boats. They set off for the cave in the hills.

"Watch your step," he called as they disappeared into the jungle. "The path is slippery today."

The giant got to the cave before the villagers did. The boy followed his father through the cave opening into a huge underground chamber.

When his eyes got used to the dim light, he could make out the great piles of salt his father had told him about. The smell was so awful he could hardly breathe.

"Fill your basket like this," said his father, crouching down at the bottom of one of the piles of salt. "Make sure you don't cause a salt slide, though."

The boy scooped up some salt with his bare hands and dropped it into his basket. He looked up at the pile of salt towering above him.

"I hope it doesn't slide down on top of me," he thought nervously. "I'd be buried alive!"

Quickly, the boy crouched down and used his hands to scoop salt like his father had shown him. He scooped and he scooped until both bamboo baskets were full. Then the boy and his father picked the baskets up, balanced them on their heads, and left the cave.

The boy stood tall so he didn't spill any of his salt as they went back down the slippery path. But then he couldn't see where he was putting his feet. Several times they got tangled in vines and he stumbled. By the time he got back to the shore, his body was sore from carrying the heavy load.

Chapter 5

A Good Idea

The boy put his basket of salt in his father's small boat. He looked up to see the giant stepping over the hills. The boy marveled at how easy it was for the huge man. He wished he had long legs like him.

"Long legs would be good for winning races and crossing mountains," he thought. Suddenly, he had an idea. He turned to the villagers who were packing the baskets into their boats.

"Why don't we make a bridge between the giant's island and our island?" he said excitedly. "Then you could get salt in all kinds of weather, and I would never get seasick again."

"No one can make a bridge that long," laughed the villagers.

"I can," said the boy, looking at the giant who was now standing on the shore.

The villagers laughed even louder.

"The boy says he can build a bridge from here to there," they said, pointing across the sea. "What a dreamer he is."

The boy's father did not like the way they laughed at his son. It was good to have dreams. "How would you make a bridge?" he asked gently.

"With the giant's legs," answered the boy. He walked over to the giant and stood beside him. He held up his hands as if measuring how long his legs were.

"Please, Giant," he called. "Can you help me make a bridge?"

The giant was puzzled. He didn't understand.

Sitting down on the sand, the giant pulled his legs up to his chest and wrapped his arms around his legs as if to hold himself together.

"How would a big giant like me be able to help a small boy like you?" he asked.

"Like this," said the boy. Quickly he made two piles of sand on the shore.

"This is your island," he explained. "And this is mine."

Then he sat on one pile of sand and stretched his legs over to the other.

"See! If you stretched out your legs, they would reach from your island to my island. Then people would come more often to get their salt."

The giant liked the idea of people coming more often to his island. A big smile spread across his face. They would bring food, and he would have more to eat.

"Tell me what to do," he said eagerly.

"Well," began the boy, "as soon as we have used up the salt we have in our baskets, we'll light a fire. The smoke will be a sign for you that we are ready."

The giant listened carefully as the boy explained how they could make a bridge. The boy's father waited patiently in his boat. He was glad the giant was interested in his son's idea.

The other villagers were strangely silent as they got ready to sail home. Perhaps the boy was on to something with his bridge idea, they thought. They wished they hadn't laughed at him.

Chapter 6

The Bridge

As soon as the villagers had used up all the salt they had collected, the boy and his father lit a fire.

The flames leapt higher and higher as the wood burned, and a trail of smoke rose into the air. The puffs of smoke told the giant that the villagers had no more salt.

Then the boy got a long bamboo stick and a bamboo ladder and looked out to sea. He shaded his eyes with his hand as he searched the horizon.

At first, the boy saw nothing. But the giant had seen the villagers' smoke signals. He stretched his long legs across the sea, his toes pointing to the sky like big, fat button mushrooms. The boy grinned when he saw the giant's feet. It was such a strange sight!

The boy waited until the giant's feet had passed over his head. Then he reached up and tapped one of the giant's feet with the bamboo stick to let him know he could put his feet down. Slowly, the giant lowered his feet until his heels touched the ground.

Quickly, the boy put the bamboo ladder against one of the giant's legs and climbed onto it. He jumped up and down, waving excitedly.

"It worked!" he shouted. "We've made a bridge."

He hoped the giant could see him. He knew he would feel him jumping up and down. "Though I'm so small, I probably feel like a grasshopper hopping on his leg!" he thought.

He looked down at the villagers who had come out of the jungle and gathered below.

"The giant's legs make a good bridge. Now we can get salt, whatever the weather," he shouted. "Well, what are you waiting for? Let's go!"

The villagers ran to get their bamboo baskets to put salt in. Suddenly, the boy remembered they needed to take food for the giant. He had seen how disappointed he was the last time when they had none.

"We must take plenty of food for the giant to thank him for his salt," said the boy. "Does anyone have any boiled rice and prawns?"

"I do," said a villager. She ran off to get a tub for the giant.

"And dried fish?" asked the boy.

"We do," said some fishermen.

Then, one by one, the villagers climbed up the ladder and followed the boy and his father along the giant's legs across the sea.

Chapter 7

Ants

The giant was happy. It was good to be able to help the villagers, and all he had to do was stretch out his legs and relax! The giant didn't realize that his large feet were resting on an ant hill.

Thousands of angry ants stormed out of their home and onto the giant's feet. At first, the giant thought something was

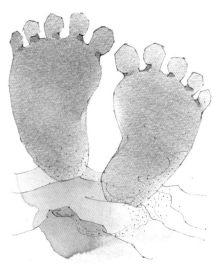

tickling him as the ants swarmed over his soles and onto his toes. He wriggled his toes, but it didn't help.

Then the ants began to bite. Each bite stung.

"Ow!" cried the giant, trying to lie still. "Ow!"

He wanted to shake the ants off, but he wasn't able to move because the villagers were walking along his legs. He wanted to scratch the bites.

"Could you please hurry?" he asked. "Ants are biting my feet."

The villagers did not believe that creatures as small as ants could annoy an enormous giant. But they did as he asked and hurried along his legs to his island. Bravely, the giant sat still until the last villager had climbed off his legs.

As the boy led them away to get salt from the cave in the hills, the giant lifted his bare feet from the ant hill. Quickly, he bent his knees and shook his feet as hard as he could over the sea. The thousands of ants looked like little seeds as they were flung into the air and then dropped down into the water.

The giant looked at his feet. The ants had left bright red marks where they had bitten him. He lowered his big feet into the sea slowly and gently. He knew if he made waves, they would wash ashore and sweep through the villages.

Then he rested his feet on the seabed and let the cool water take the sting out of the bites.

While he waited for the villagers to return, he ate their gifts of boiled rice with prawns and dried fish.

"I must ask them to bring dried squid next time," he thought. He closed his eyes and thought about the cave. This was the first time he hadn't waited outside it to make sure no one was hurt. He hoped there were no salt slides.

The giant was asleep with his feet still on the seabed when the villagers returned with their bamboo baskets filled with salt. He woke with a start.

"How are the ant bites?" the villagers asked the giant. The giant chuckled.

"Well, there are a lot fewer ants on your island now, thanks to me," he laughed.

The villagers laughed with him. They liked this enormous man. They wouldn't go back to their island just yet. They'd stay a while and keep him company. Besides, there was no bridge to cross while his feet were soaking in the sea.

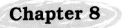

Chapter 8

Salty Sea

At sunset, the villagers decided to return to their own island. The giant stretched his legs across the sea again. He lifted the villagers and their baskets of salt onto his legs and said goodbye.

He was sad to see the people go, especially the boy. He hadn't realized how lonely he was on the island by himself.

As the villagers walked back home along his legs, the giant felt something crawl over his feet. At first, he thought he was being tickled. But then he felt a bite and another and another.

"Oh no!" cried the giant. "It's the ants again!"

Once again, the giant couldn't shake off the ants. Once again, the giant politely asked the villagers to hurry. But this time the villagers were carrying bamboo baskets full of salt on their heads. It was much harder for them to move quickly.

"Faster," begged the poor giant. "Faster!"

He wondered how much longer he would be able to bear the pain of the ants biting his feet. The villagers held on tightly to their baskets and ran along the giant's legs, but they were tired from carrying their heavy loads. They gasped for air and wobbled from side to side.

But the giant could not wait for the villagers to get back to their island. With a roar of pain, he lifted his legs into the air. He shook his feet roughly to get rid of the annoying ants.

The villagers were taken by surprise. They screamed, dropped their baskets of salt, and let them tumble into the sea. The villagers were thrown into the water.

"Save us!" they yelled.

When the giant saw what he had done, he was very upset. He had not meant to harm the villagers. He reached across the sea and plucked them out of the water and sat them on his knees to dry, while he soaked his feet in the sea again.

The villagers could see their bamboo baskets floating on the top of the water below them. They were empty. All the salt they had collected from the giant's cave had spilled into the water.

And that is why the sea is salty!